THE DREAM-HOUSE

The Dream-House
by Fu-Ding Cheng

Cover design by Marjoram Productions
Cover painting by Fu-Ding Cheng

For information write:

Hampton Roads Publishing Company, Inc.
1125 Stoney Ridge Road
Charlottesville, VA 22902

Or call: 804-296-2772
FAX: 804-296-5096
e-mail: hrpc@hrpub.com
Web site: www.hrpub.com

If you are unable to order this book from your local bookseller, you may order directly from the publisher.
Quantity discounts for organizations are available. Call 1-800-766-8009, toll-free.

Library of Congress Catalog Card Number: 00-102568

ISBN 1-57174-186-0

10 9 8 7 6 5 4 3 2 1

Printed on acid-free paper in China

For children of all ages

Who dream of homes filled with magic.

ACKNOWLEDGEMENTS

To Spirit that inspired this book

and

To the many friends and colleagues whose support, ideas, and talents
helped bring it to life including Linda Jacobson, Renee Cho, Art Ellis,
Marilyn Ferguson, Judith Samuels, Scott Canty, Brooke Breton, Alex Cheng,
Laurel Vanderlin, Bronwyn Jones, Miguel Ruiz, the L.A. Circle of Fire, and
to Grace Pedalino, Jane Hagaman, and Robert Friedman of Hampton Roads.

Thank you!

Once upon a time, I was a house made

out of dreams. Seeking adventure,

I roamed the heavens and floated with the wind.

Free to go anywhere, I wondered . . .

"Where shall I go?"

I drifted down a sunbeam to a meadow
filled with laughter. There was a young

family with a little boy named Billy. As
I watched, I knew we belonged together. With them,
I could be more than a house. I could be a *home!*

But how could I get to know them?

I floated around and around them, and even *through* them until they all began dreaming . . . about me!

Very soon, my wish came true. *I* was being built! A wood

skeleton made me strong, glass windows let me see,

and a big fireplace showed the warmth of my heart.

Before I knew it, I was finished. Complete. A rock foundation kept me solid with the earth, skylights opened me to the heavens. I felt strong, beautiful, and proud.

But still, something was missing.

I was lonely. But when Billy and his family moved

in and began living inside me, I came alive! I was home.

I loved protecting them.  When the days

became too hot and sticky, I cooled them down

with plenty of shade . . .

 . . . and when nights became windy and cold, I kept them warm and cozy within my walls.

From the beginning, Billy was full of surprises. One night,

he was secretly playing ball *inside* me. I could just feel an

accident coming. And then it happened!

The cold blew right in. Billy and his dad began plugging

in more and more electric heaters. My wires began to burn!

I got scared. What's happening to me?

Suddenly everything turned black!

When I awoke, noise and workmen were everywhere.

Billy and his dad were giving me a brand new picture

window. Billy polished it, promising he'd never be so

careless again. But knowing Billy,

I wondered . . .

One summer it got so hot and stuffy I couldn't breathe. Billy tried to help by opening my windows to let the breeze in.

Then the meadow caught on fire.

Red-hot embers sparked in the air.

Suddenly, flames broke out over me. I was

on fire! Billy ran to me. Everyone shouted at him,

"Keep back, Billy! Keep back!"

But Billy wouldn't listen. He ran to me with the garden

hose and saved my life!

That day he became my hero.

When Billy got older, he met a girl named Marie.

Day and night he walked around

in a daze thinking about her.

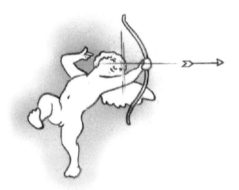

I began worrying about him.

Then he got to know her. He was so full of love and

surprises that he charmed her just like he had charmed me.

Billy and Marie fell in love.

I wasn't surprised when they got married. I felt honored

to be the setting for their beautiful wedding ceremony.

But my favorite part was that they got *me* for a present!

Billy's parents moved nearby, knowing

that we would all be happy together.

As Billy and Marie's family grew bigger,

so did I! When they got a new baby,

I got a new room. Through the years

I went through many changes, all lovingly built by

Billy's own hands. He was so full of surprises I never

knew what to expect.

But some things never changed. The favorite spot for the whole family was always around my fireplace. Here they would tell wonderful stories and make up magical games.

 Winter, spring, summer, and fall—the seasons came and went. The children grew up and left home so that once again, it was just me, Billy and Marie.

Some of my favorite times came when Billy's parents and his children came home during holidays. One time Billy decorated me so beautifully that I burst out and joined everyone in song!

After many wonderful years, Billy put up a *For Sale* sign and sadly said goodbye to me. I was shocked to see him drive off. I wondered if I would ever see him again.

I was so sad and lonely, I felt like sinking into the ground.

Other nice people lived in me, but they didn't always take good care of me. Soon no one came around at all.

I began falling apart.

After awhile, I lost my roof. Storms came right in and beat me to pieces. I was terrified. But then a wonderful thing happened. The rain washed my sorrows away, the sun warmed up my heart, and the wind blew my imagination free.

That's when I heard a voice calling me from the stars. "*Home is where the heart is, and yours has always loved adventure. It's time to let go of the past and begin anew. Come, come . . .*"

Suddenly I remembered who I really am. I'm much

more than wood, stone, or glass. I'm made out of *dreams!*

If I'd just let go of my old walls I could

join the voice in the stars.

So once upon a time, again, I roamed the heavens and floated with the wind. Following the voice, I found a new wonderful family . . . but that's another story.

. . . DREAM-HOUSE ON THE MOON

ABOUT THE AUTHOR

Fu-Ding Cheng began his multifaceted career as an architect and painter, later turning to make films and videos. His innovative, prize-winning films have been seen in dozens of film festivals in Europe, the United States and Asia.

His on-going series of films "Zen-Tales for the Urban Explorer" include *Spirit of the Dream-House*, and *The Winged Cage* which won a Gold Prize at the Houston International Film Festival. His paintings for *Dream-House* were featured in an Art Exhibit at the Municipal Art Gallery of Los Angeles.

He is now working on other projects based on his spiritual/shamanic practices, including *The Book of Altars* and a mystical adventure story for a film, *A Time of Miracles*. For more information about his multifaceted involvements, visit his web site at www.liquidlightproductions.com.

Hampton Roads Publishing Company is dedicated to providing quality children's books that
stimulate the intellect, teach valuable lessons, and allow our children's spirits to grow.
We have created our line of Young Spirit Books for the evolving human spirit of our children.
Give your children Young Spirit Books—their key to a whole new world!

Hampton Roads Publishing Company

. . . for the evolving human spirit

Hampton Roads Publishing Company publishes books on a variety of subjects including
metaphysics, health, complementary medicine, visionary fiction, and other related topics.

For a copy of our latest catalog,
call toll-free, 800-766-8009,
or send your name and address to:

Hampton Roads Publishing Company, Inc.
1125 Stoney Ridge Road
Charlottesville, VA 22902
e-mail: hrpc@hrpub.com
www.hrpub.com